Amazing 3D Mazes
Activity Book
For Kids 7-12

- RUSS FOCUS -

ISBN-13: 978-1723500824   ISBN-10: 1723500828

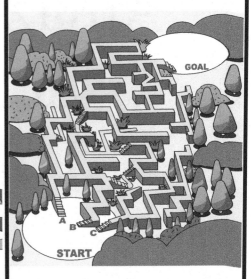

SAMPLE 3D MAZE ACTIVITY 17 of 40 PAGES

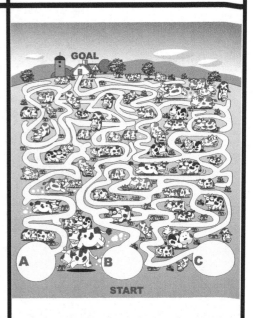

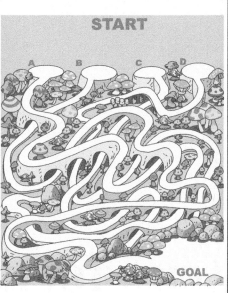

GOAL

A

B

C

START

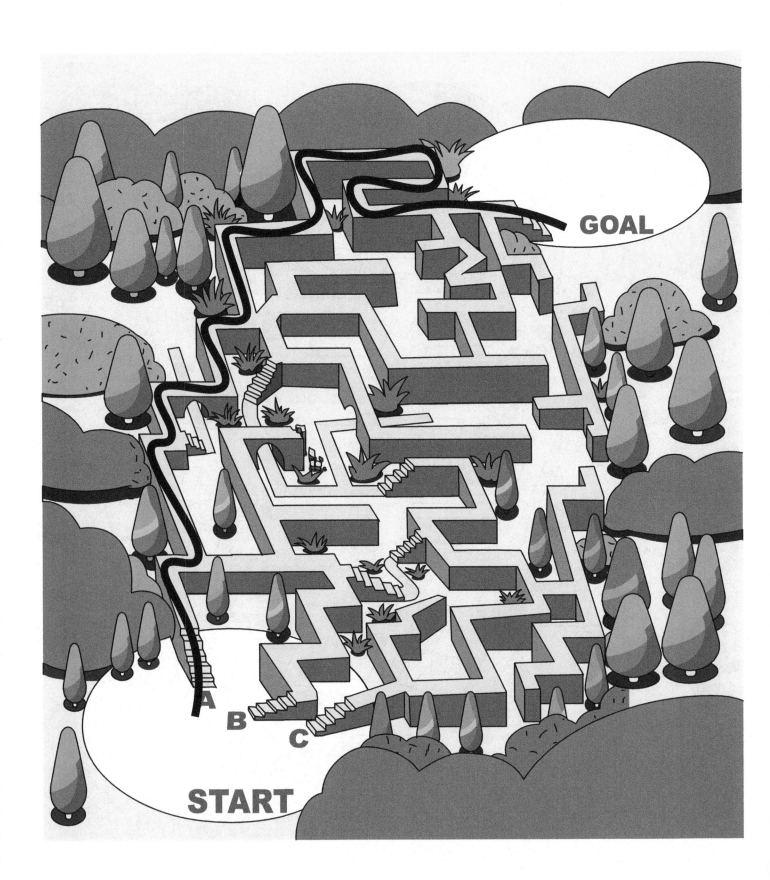

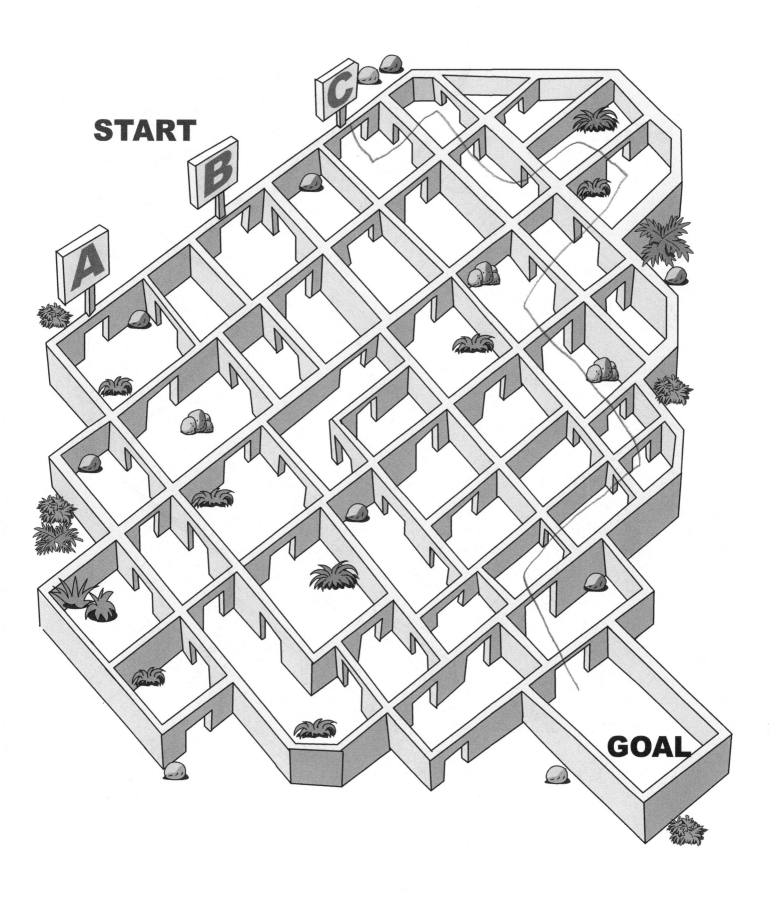

START

A

B

C

GOAL

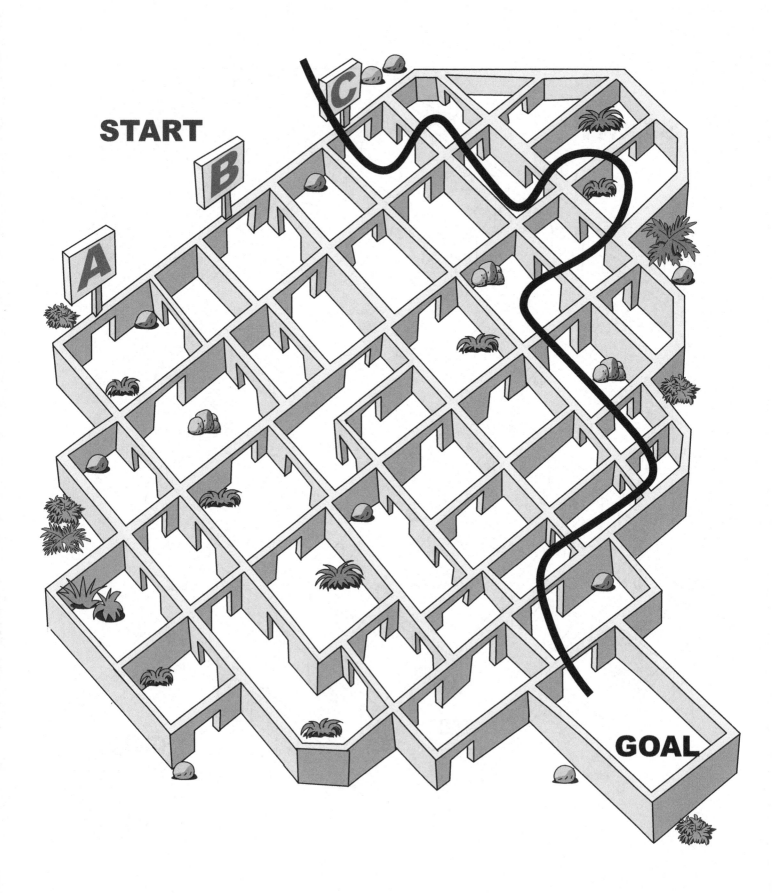

START

A　　**B**　　**C**

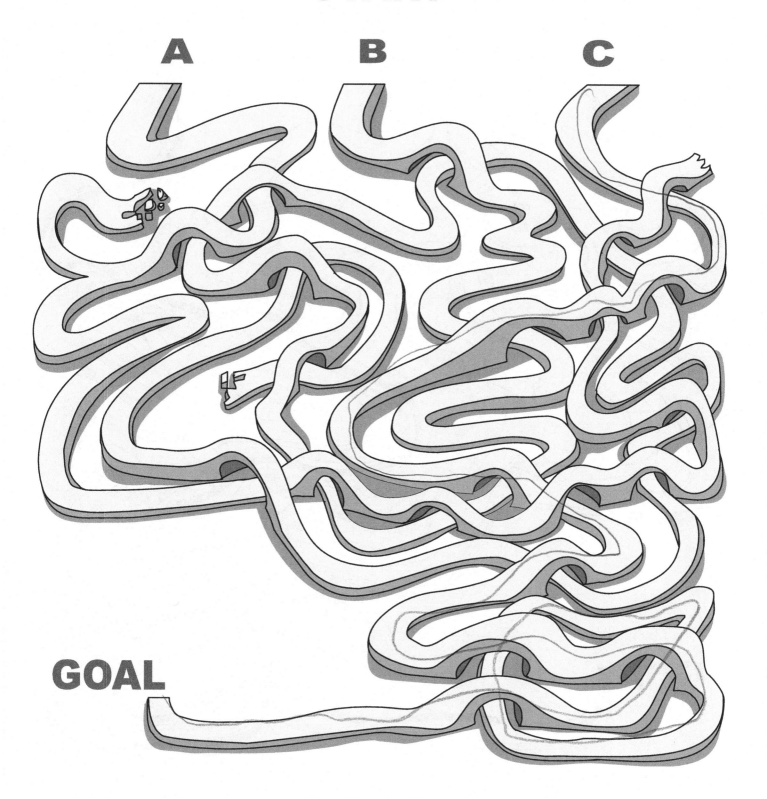

GOAL

START

A   B   C

GOAL

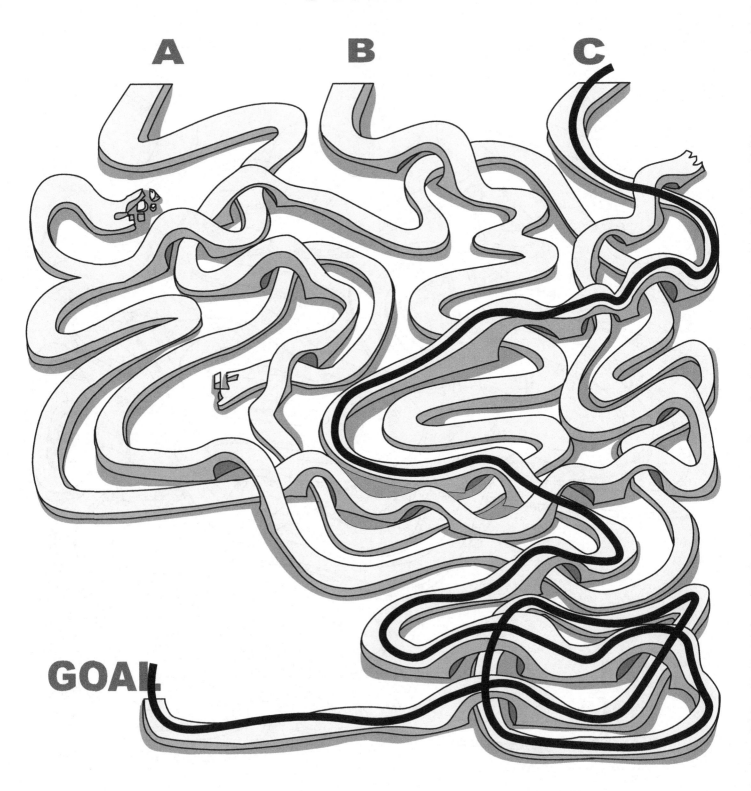

START

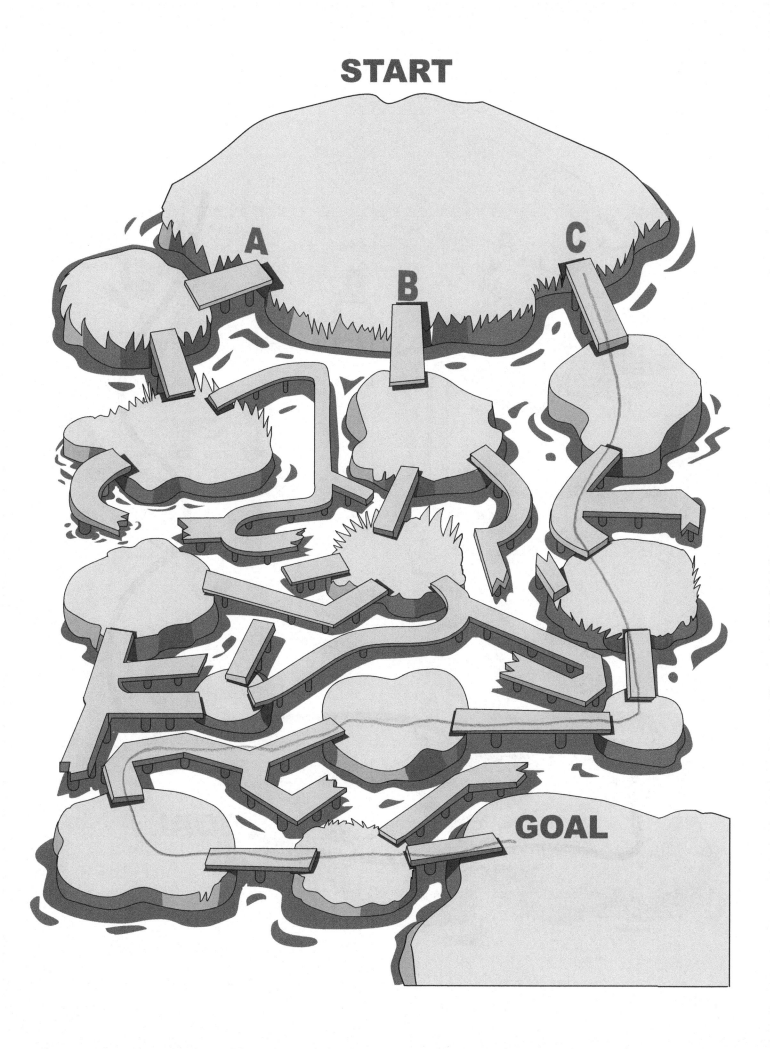

GOAL

START

A   B   C

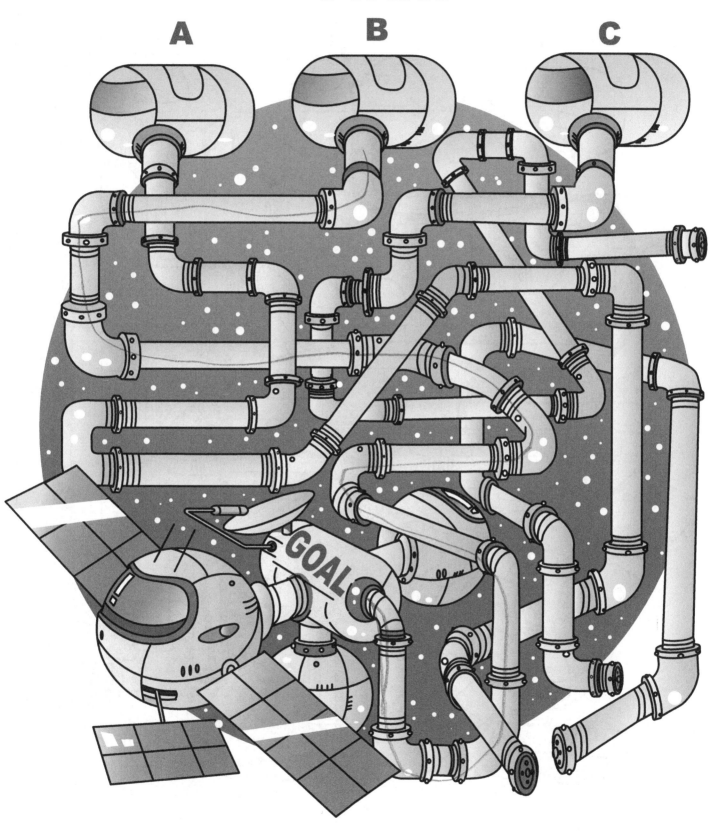

GOAL

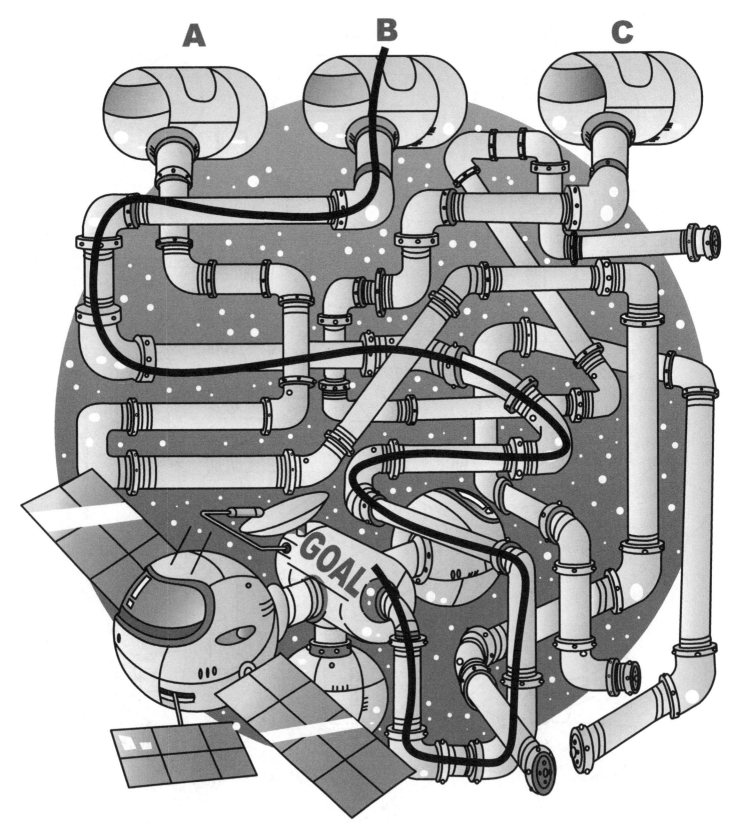

GOAL

START

GOAL

A B C

START

GOAL

A

B

C

START

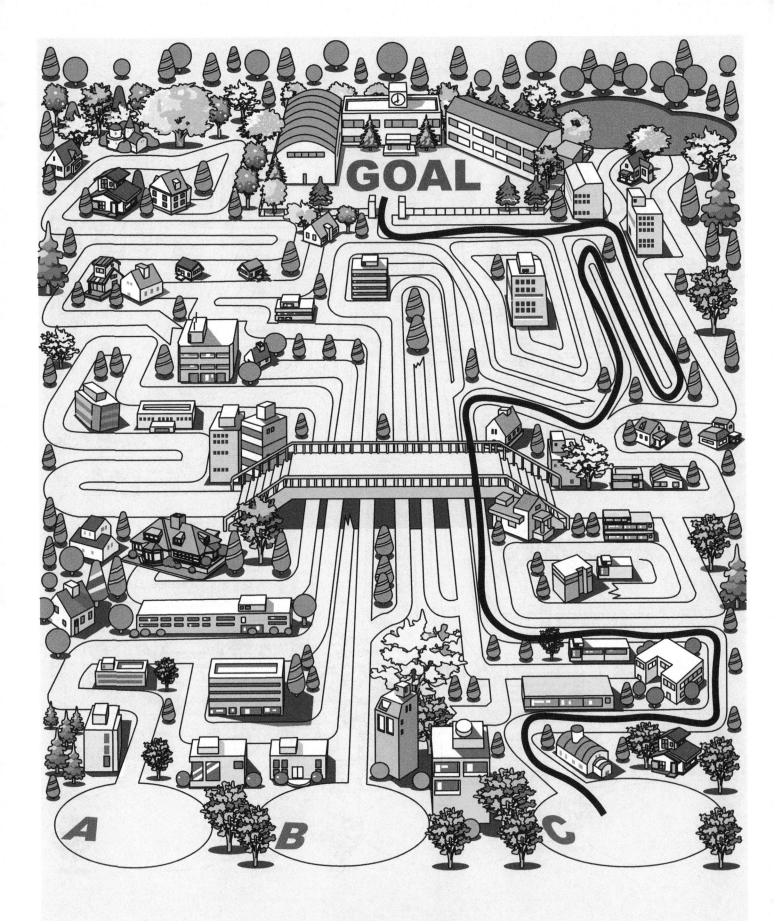

GOAL

A

B

C

START

GOAL

A

B

C

START

GOAL

A

B

C

START

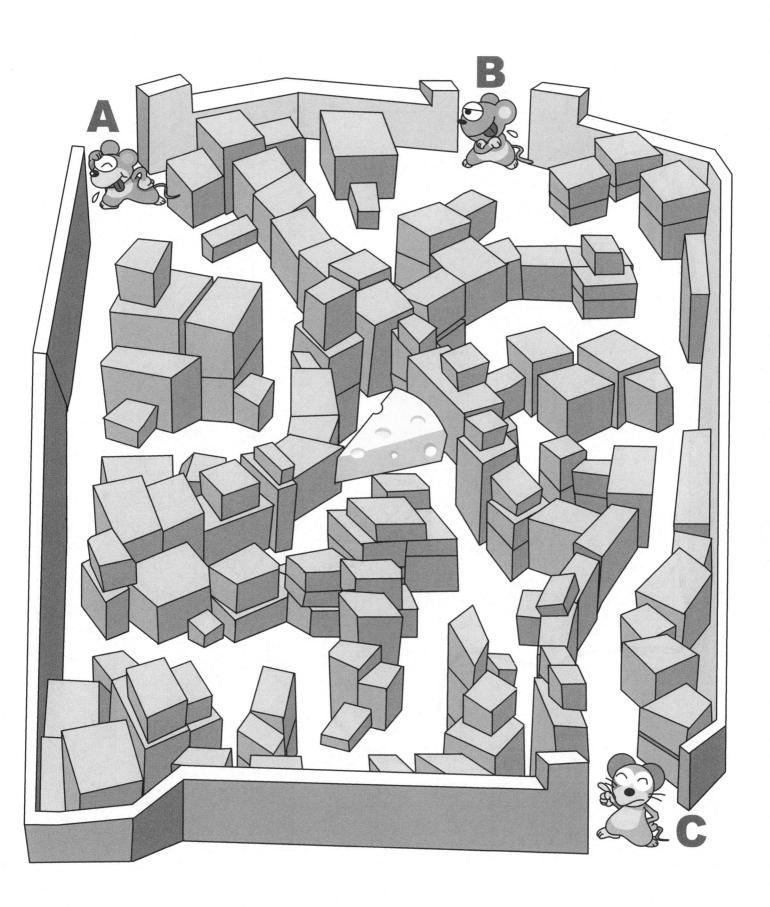

GOAL

A
B
C

START

GOAL

A
B
C

START

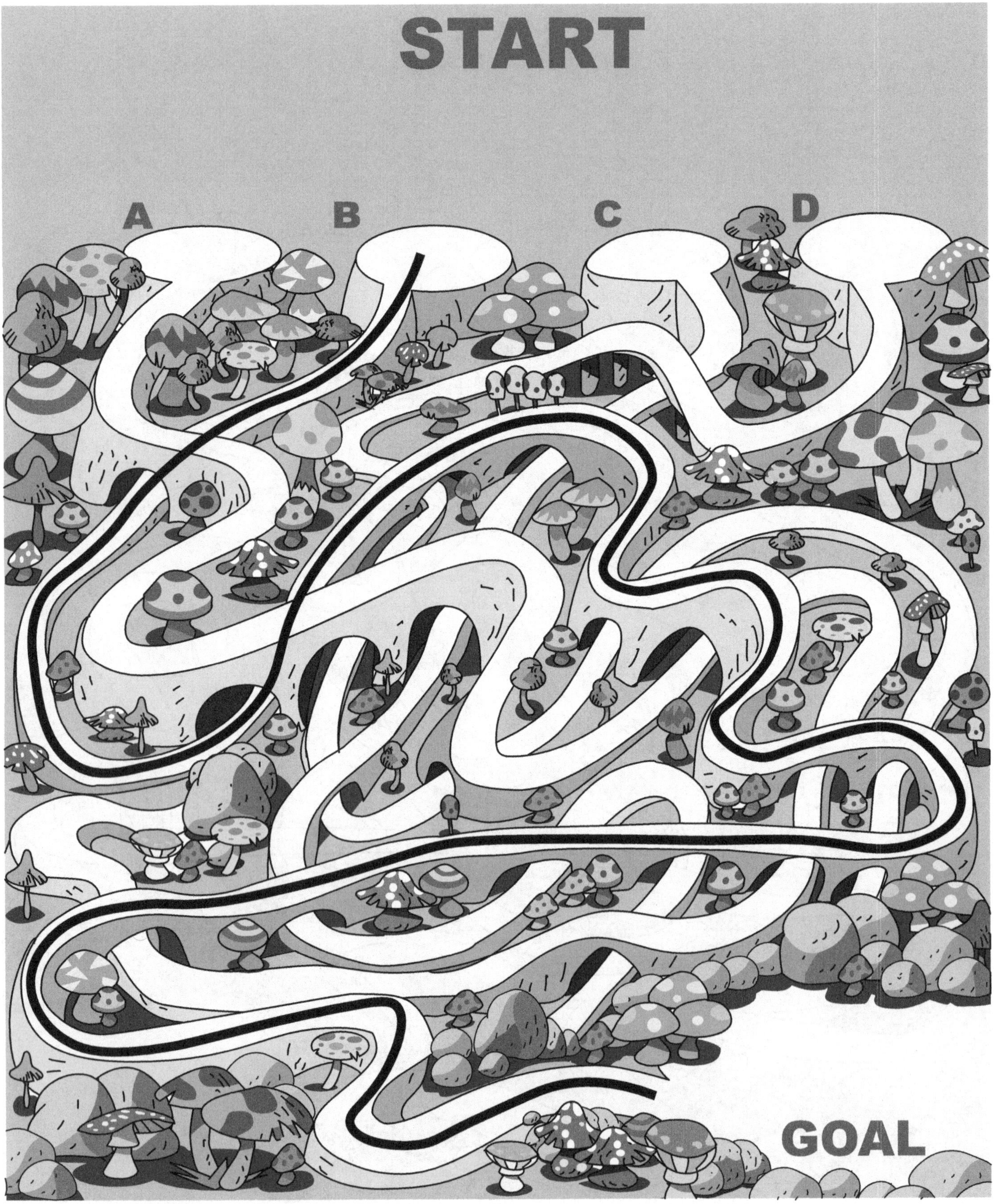
START
A
B
C
D
GOAL

GOAL

A

B

START

C

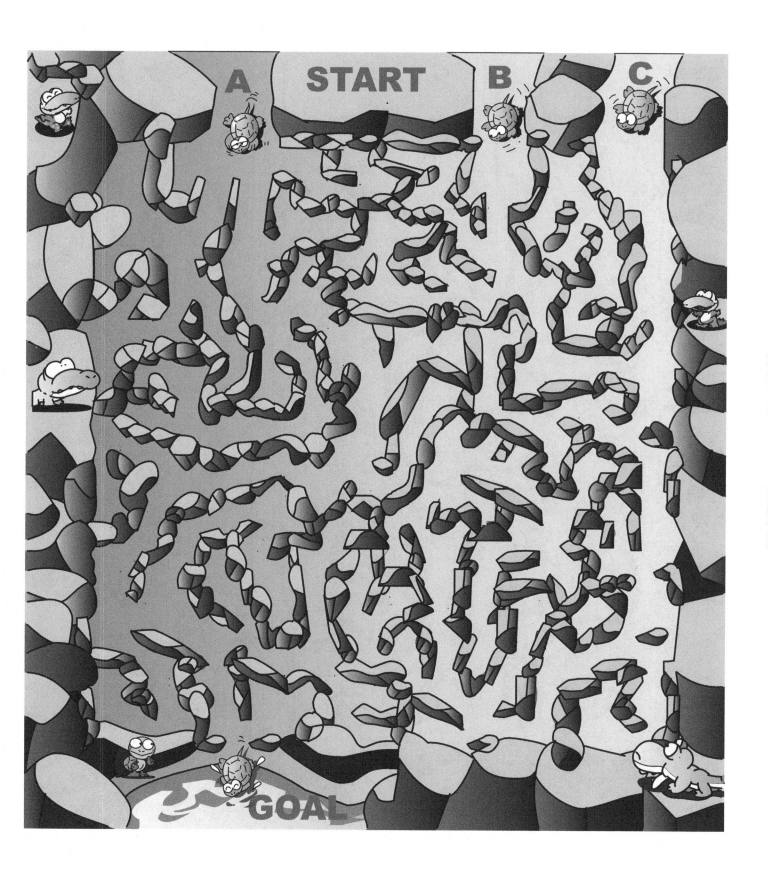

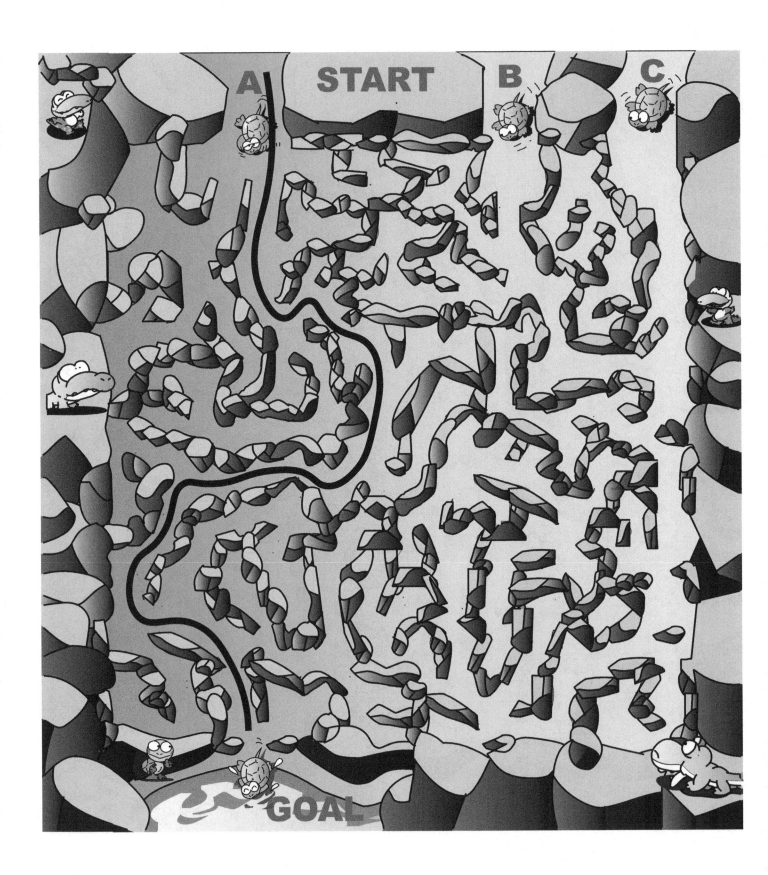

START

A

B

C

GOAL

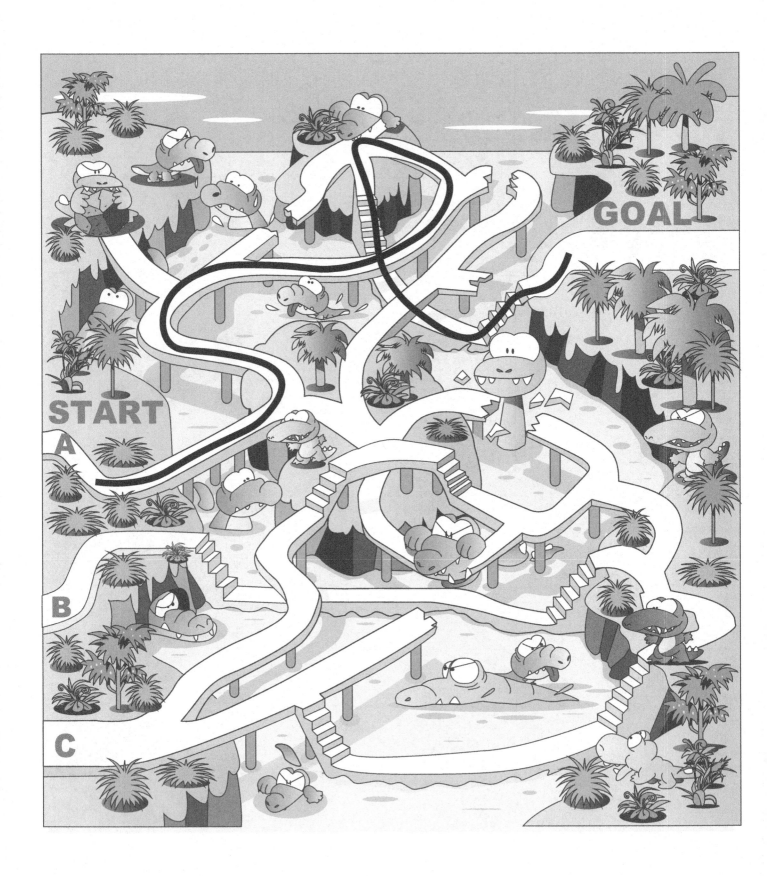

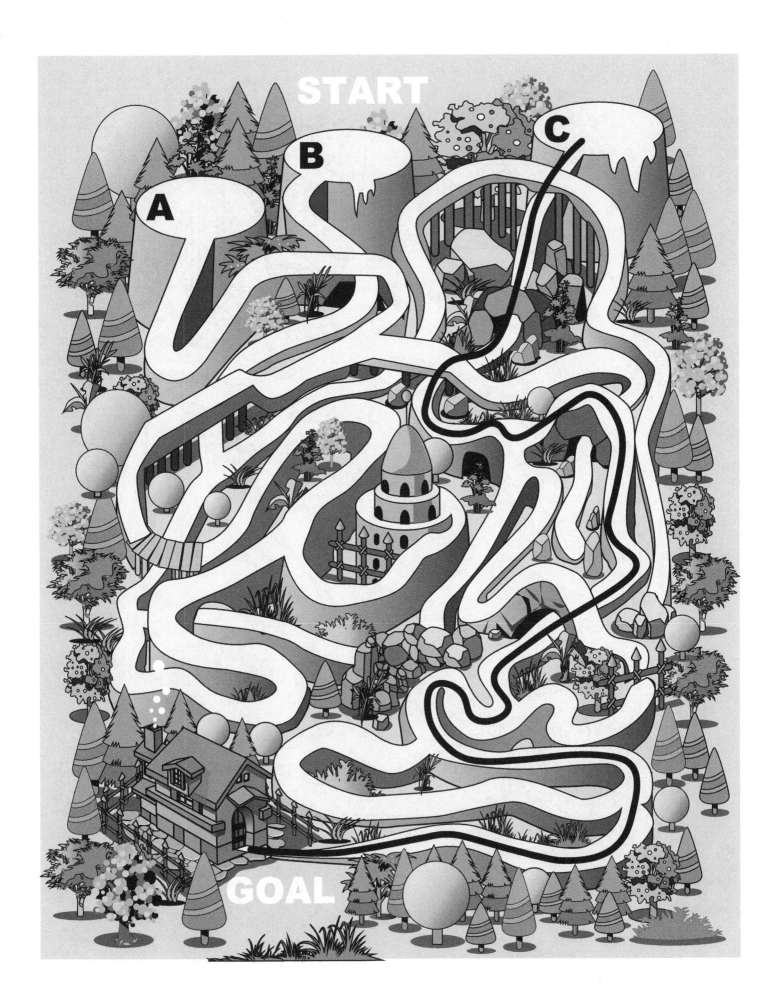

GOAL

START

A　B　C

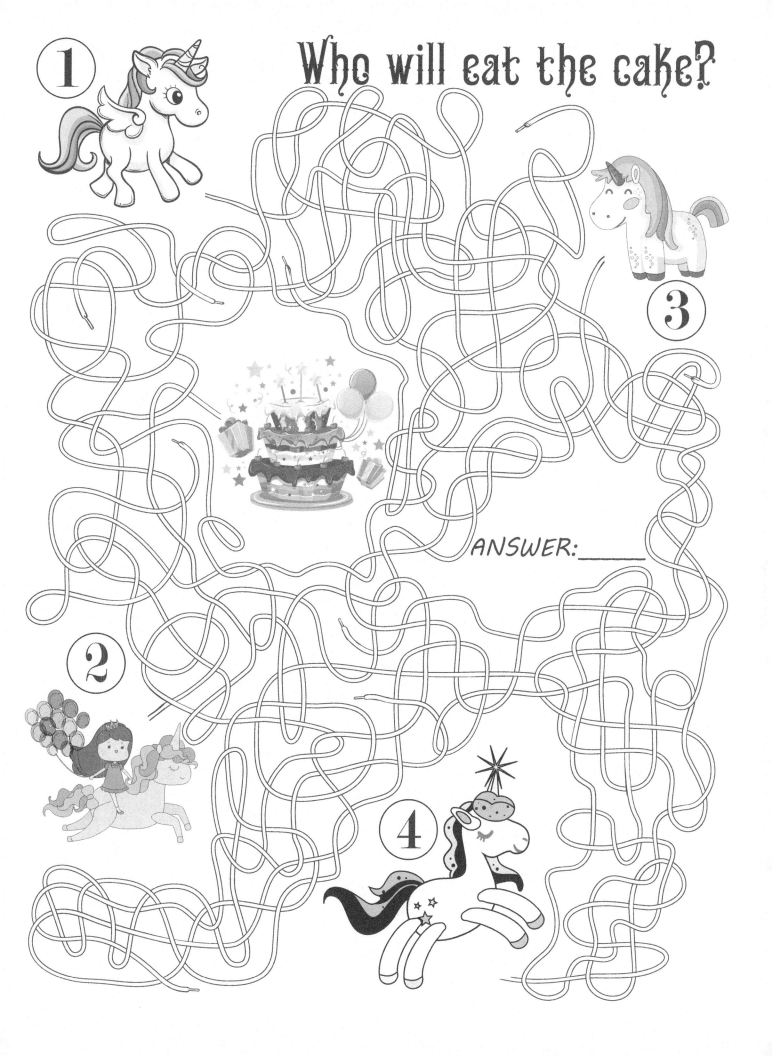

Who will eat the cake?

ANSWER:_____

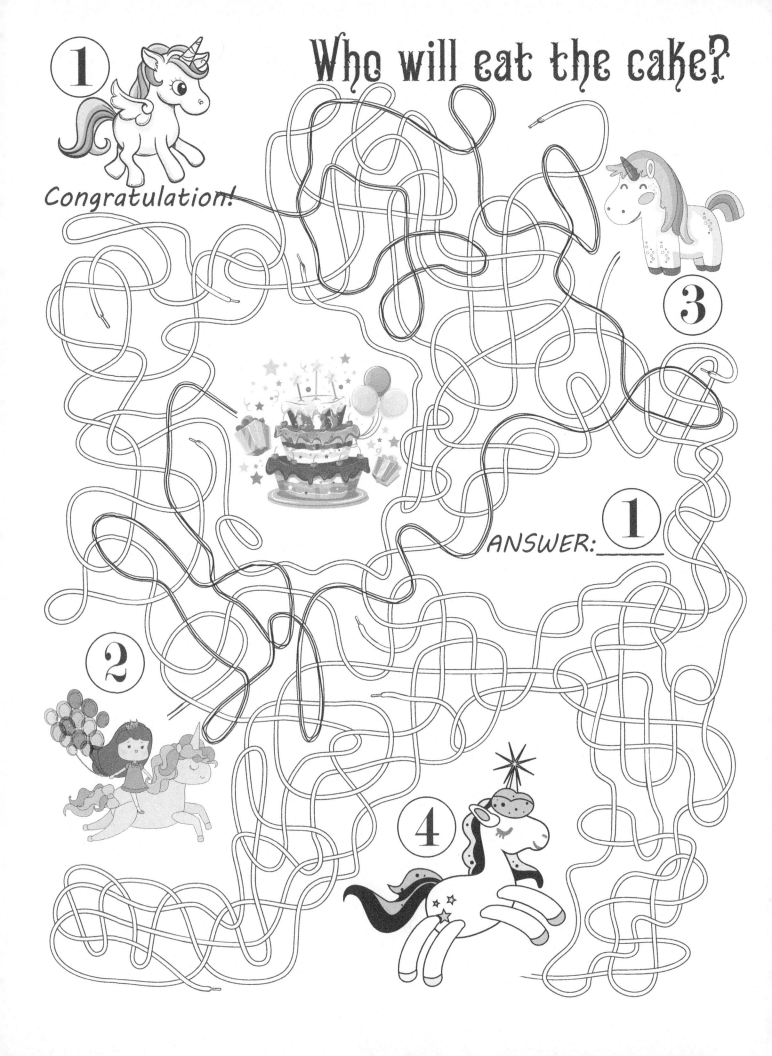

Who will eat the cake?

1 Congratulation!

3

ANSWER: **1**

2

4

GOAL

A

B

START

C

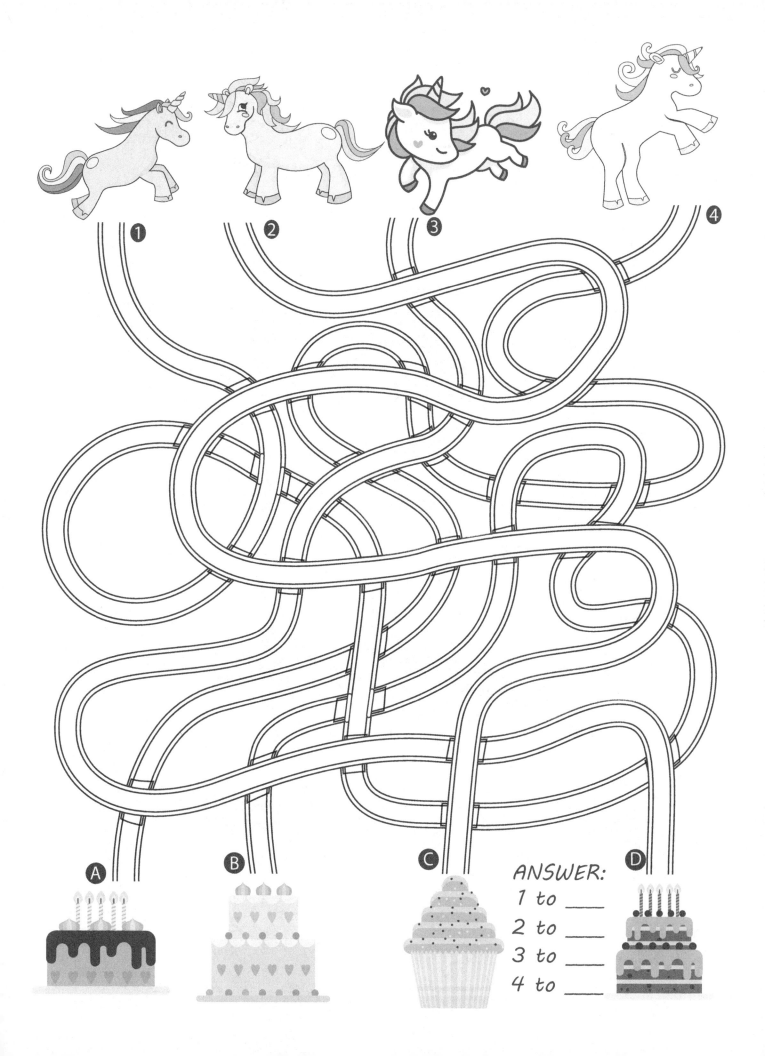

ANSWER:
1 to ____
2 to ____
3 to ____
4 to ____

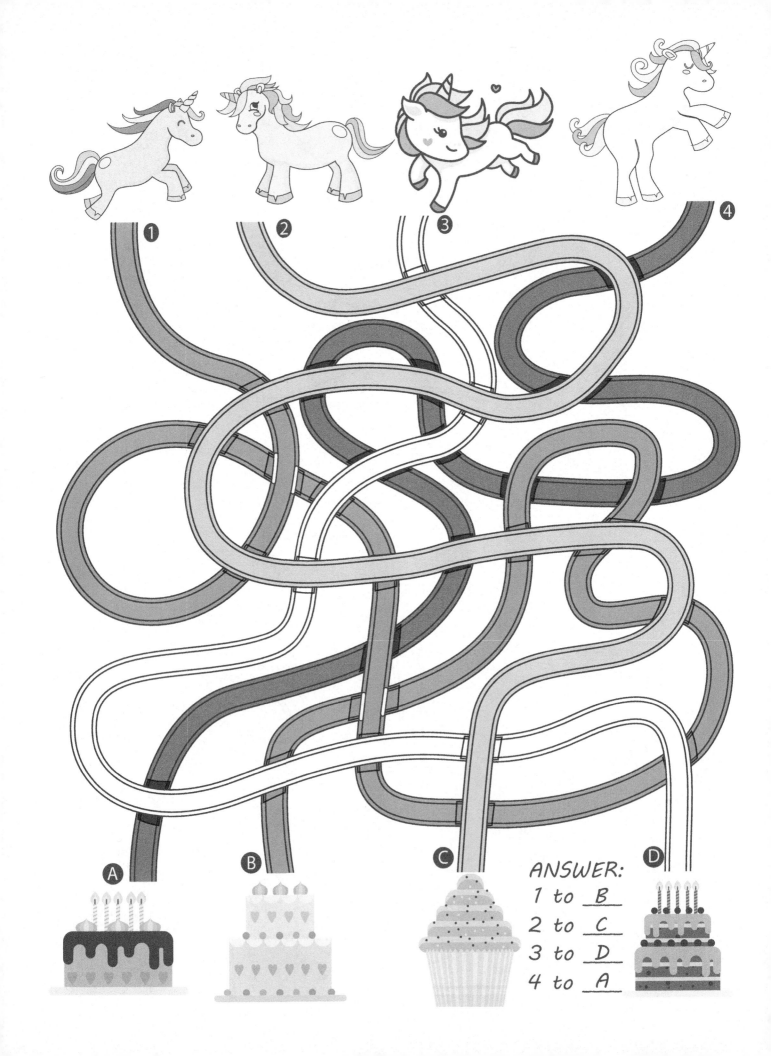

ANSWER:
1 to _B_
2 to _C_
3 to _D_
4 to _A_

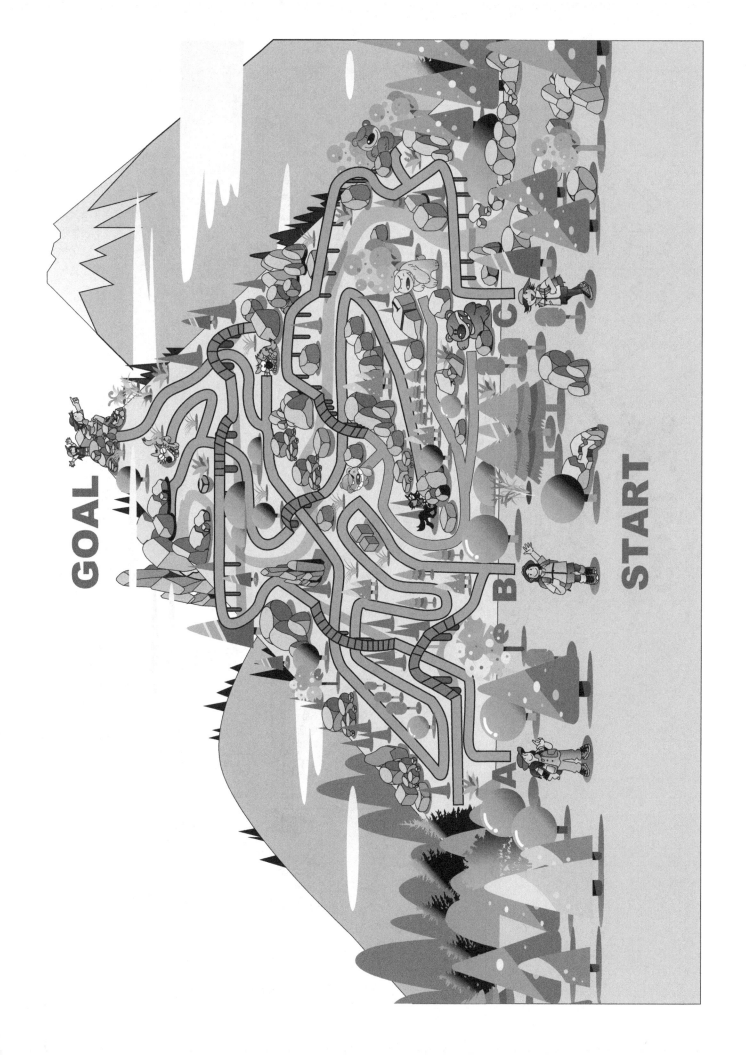

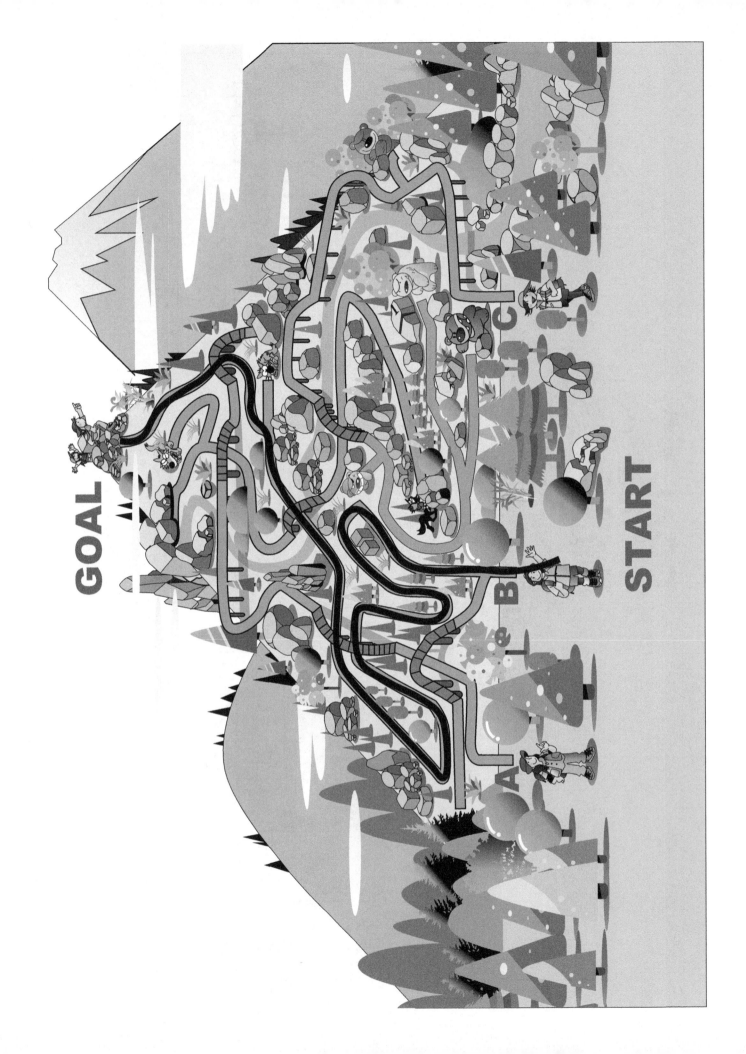

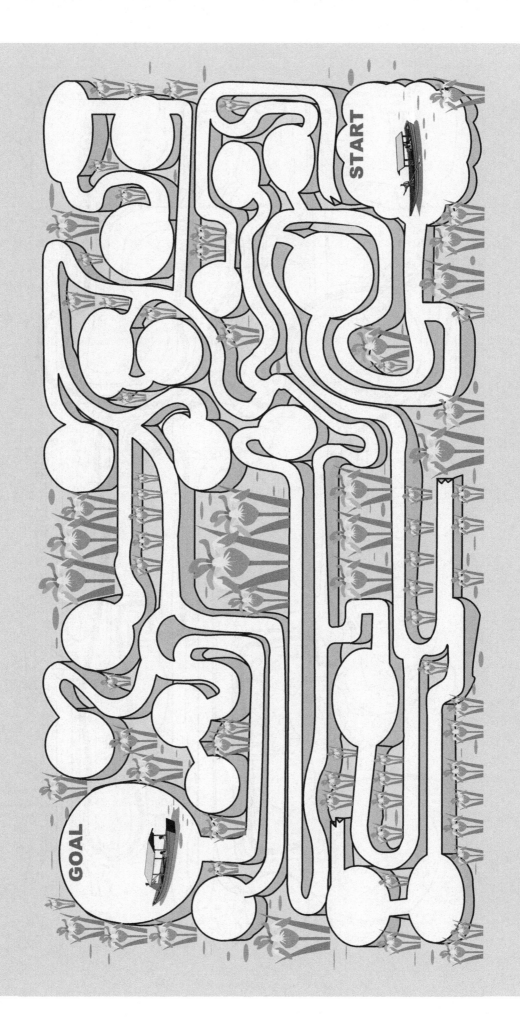

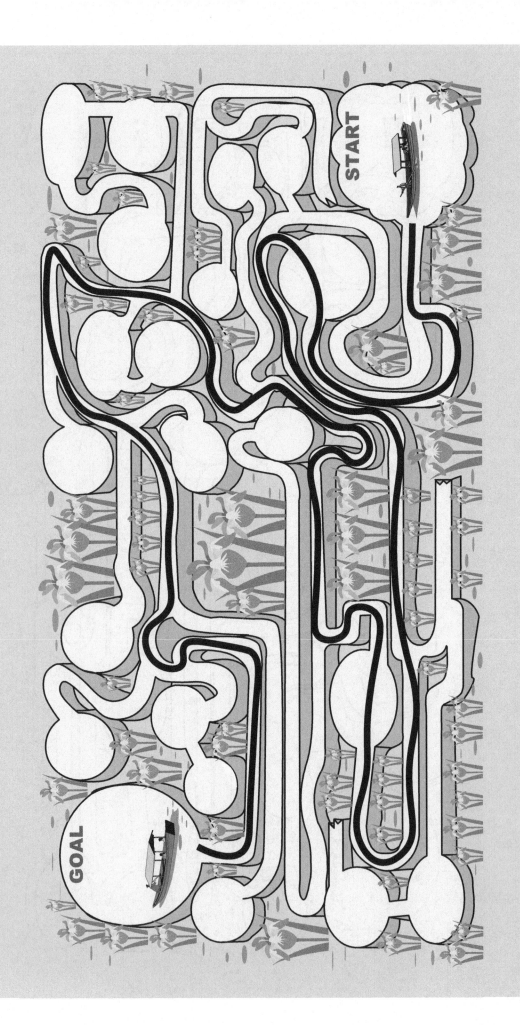